Higher

Art & Design

2005 Exam
Paper 1 Practical Assignment
Paper 2

2006 Exam
Paper 1 Practical Assignment
Paper 2

2007 Exam

2008 Exam

Leckie × Leckie

First exam published in 2005.

Published by Leckie & Leckie Ltd, 3rd Floor, 4 Queen Street, Edinburgh EH2 1JE

tel: 0131 220 6831 fax: 0131 225 9987 enquiries@leckieandleckie.co.uk www.leckieandleckie.co.uk

ISBN 978-1-84372-670-8

A CIP Catalogue record for this book is available from the British Library.

Leckie & Leckie is a division of Huveaux plc.

Leckie & Leckie is grateful to the copyright holders, as credited at the back of the book, for permission to use their material. Every effort has been made to trace the copyright holders and to obtain their permission for the use of copyright material. Leckie & Leckie will gladly receive information enabling them to rectify any error or omission in subsequent editions.

[BLANK PAGE]

X003/301

NATIONAL
QUALIFICATIONS
2005

ART AND DESIGN
HIGHER
Paper 1
Practical Assignment

The Practical Examinations for the 2005 examination diet may take place at the centre's discretion on the most convenient date in the period from Monday 25 April until Friday 6 May inclusive.

Time allowed: 3 hours

50 marks are assigned to this paper.

Maximum sizes: Two-dimensional work: A2.
                            Three-dimensional work: 30 cm in greatest dimension.

Any medium except oil paint may be used.

SCOTTISH
QUALIFICATIONS
AUTHORITY

GENERAL INSTRUCTIONS

Base your work for the Practical Assignment on your Expressive Activity folio **or** your Design Activity folio.

In the examination room you may refer to:

- Design **or** Expressive Folio of work
- Practical Assignment Form

You may use any three-dimensional source materials identified in the folio you have selected.

You will be allowed up to 20 minutes after the examination to assemble your work on the maximum number of sheets (2 × A2 sheets).

This extension time is not to be used for producing examination work.

Note: Copying of drawings and/or photographs from your folio by means such as TRACING, LIGHT BOXES, DIGITAL CAMERAS and PHOTOCOPYING **will not be permitted during the examination**. This exclusion also includes images and/or information copied from folios and stored on disk and/or CD.

Select **either** SECTION A **or** SECTION B.

SECTION A

Expressive Activity

Task

You should produce practical work which demonstrates your ability to develop and/or refine work carried out in your Expressive folio. This could take the form of new and further developments from your stimulus and might include extending ideas leading to alternative outcome(s) not fully explored within the work of your folio.

Remember that work produced for this Assignment should relate directly to your EXPRESSIVE folio theme and must develop, not copy, work already done. Further investigative work, such as analytical drawing, is not appropriate in this Assignment.

The following suggestions are provided to help you get started:

- produce work based on the stimulus or sources used by you but not fully explored in the work of your Expressive folio
- produce work which emphasises a different style or approach to your chosen theme.

Work should be on a maximum of **two** A2 sheets or equivalent three-dimensional work. You may use any suitable media, materials or process.

SECTION B

Design Activity

Task

You should produce practical work which demonstrates an alternative approach or approaches to work carried out in your Design folio. This could take the form of new and further developments from your brief and might include extending Design ideas not fully explored within the work of your folio.

Remember that work produced for this Assignment should relate to your DESIGN brief and design folio and must develop, not copy, work already done. Further investigative work, such as analytical drawing, is not appropriate in this Assignment.

The following suggestions are provided to help you get started:

- develop design ideas which you considered but did not fully explore in the work of your Design folio

- reconsider your solution and suggest further modifications and/or changes to improve it.

Work should be on a maximum of **two** A2 sheets or equivalent three-dimensional work. You may use any suitable media, materials or process.

[END OF QUESTION PAPER]

[BLANK PAGE]

X003/302

NATIONAL QUALIFICATIONS 2005	TUESDAY, 31 MAY 1.00PM – 3.00PM	ART AND DESIGN HIGHER Paper 2

There are **two** sections to this paper, Section 1—Art Studies; and Section 2—Design Studies.

Each section is worth 40 marks.

Candidates should attempt questions as follows:

In SECTION 1 answer **ONE full question** (parts (*a*) and (*b*)) and **ONE part (*a*) only** of any other question

and

In SECTION 2 answer **ONE full question** (parts (*a*) and (*b*)) and **ONE part (*a*) only** of any other question.

You may use sketches to illustrate your answers.

SCOTTISH
QUALIFICATIONS
AUTHORITY

©

SECTION 1—ART STUDIES

Instructions

Answer **ONE full question**, (parts (*a*) and (*b*)), and **ONE part (*a*) only** of any other question.

Frida Kahlo   *Diego on My Mind (Self-Portrait as Tehuana*[1] *Indian)* (1943)
oil on canvas (75 × 59·7 cm)

[1] *Tehuana*—a native of a southern region of Mexico

1. Portraiture

Marks

(*a*) Explain to what extent you consider this to be an accurate self portrait of the artist or an example of imaginative painting. Refer to the artist's use of visual elements and her symbolic use of images.

10

(*b*) Referring to examples of portraiture by **two** artists from different movements or periods, explain why you consider the works to be successful. How important are these artists in the development of portraiture?

20

SECTION 1—ART STUDIES (continued)

Paula Rego   *The Dance* (1988) acrylic on paper on canvas (213·4 × 274·3 cm)

Marks

2. Figure Composition

(a) Discuss the composition of this painting. Comment on the methods used by the artist to create strong visual impact. What is your opinion of the painting?   **10**

(b) Discuss examples of figure composition by **two** artists from different movements or periods. Outline the methods used by the artists to create their work. Explain to what extent the examples are typical of their style or associated movement.   **20**

[Turn over

SECTION 1—ART STUDIES (continued)

Henri Fantin-Latour   *Still Life with Vase of Hydrangeas and Ranunculus* (1866)
oil on canvas (73 × 59·6 cm)

Marks

3. Still Life

(*a*) Analyse this painting in terms of the artist's choice of subject matter. Refer to composition, media handling and his use of visual elements. What is your opinion of this painting?

10

(*b*) Select **two** artists from different movements or periods. Referring to at least one example by each of them, explain differences and/or similarities in their approach to still life. To what extent are the artists influential in the development of still life?

20

SECTION 1—ART STUDIES (continued)

Raoul Dufy   *The Wheatfield* (1929) oil on canvas (130 × 162 cm)

Marks

4.   Natural Environment

(a)   Discuss the methods used by Dufy to create depth and atmosphere in this painting. Refer to his use of visual elements and painting style. What is your opinion of this painting?

10

(b)   Select **two** artists from different movements or periods whose works respond to the natural environment. Discuss what each artist has communicated to you about the environment. Comment on their choice of subject matter and their working methods. Why are they considered to be important artists?

20

[Turn over

SECTION 1—ART STUDIES (continued)

Lyonel Feininger *Market Church at Evening* (1930) oil on canvas (102 × 80·5 cm)

Marks

5. Built Environment

(a) Discuss the artist's treatment of this subject. Comment on his use of line, colour and tone. Identify aspects of the painting you admire and/or those you consider to be less successful. In doing so, give reasons.

10

(b) Referring to the work of **two** artists from different movements or periods discuss their treatment of the built environment. Comment on their choice of subject matter and working methods. To what extent is their work typical of their associated movements or styles?

20

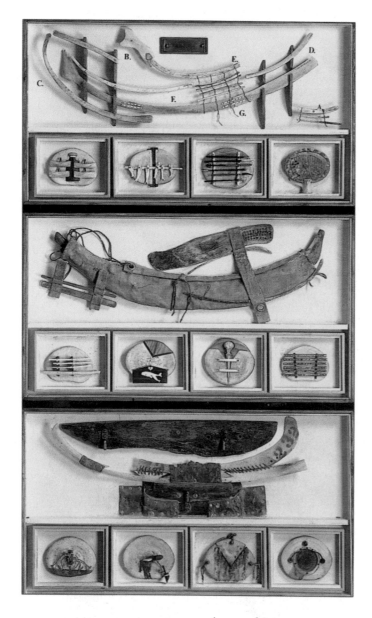

Will Maclean *Leviathan*[1] *Elegy*[2] (1982)
painted whalebone and found objects[3] (203 × 137 × 10 cm)

[1]*Leviathan*—something of enormous size and power

[2]*Elegy*—a sorrowful poem

[3]This work is constructed from found, carved and painted objects assembled in three boxes.

Marks

6. Fantasy and Imagination

(*a*) Discuss the content of this work and the artist's method of presenting it. Comment on at least **two** of the following:

form, scale, materials, colour, composition.

What, in your opinion, is the artist communicating to us in this piece? **10**

(*b*) Discuss examples by **two** artists from different movements or periods whose work is within the theme of fantasy and imagination. Comment on the sources of inspiration and methods used by the artists to produce their work. Explain why these artists are considered to be important. **20**

Instructions

Answer **ONE full question**, (parts (*a*) and (*b*)), and **ONE part (*a*) only** of any other question.

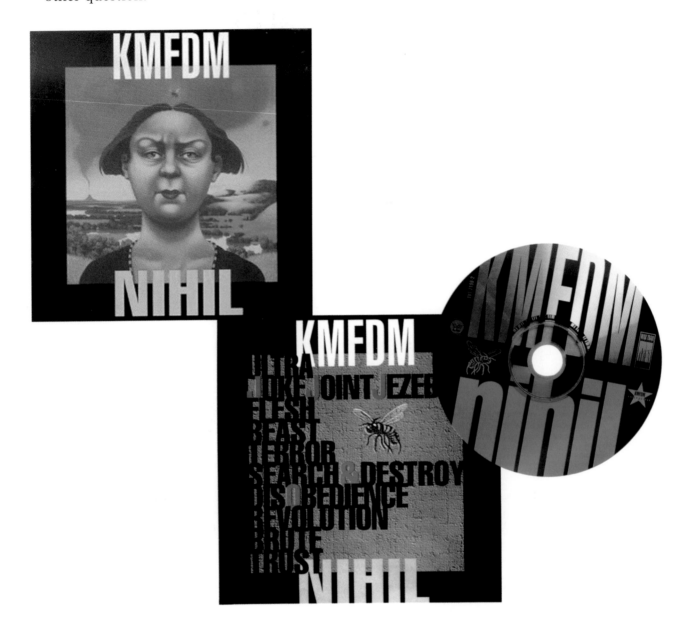

Nihil[1]—CD design for band called KMFDM (1995)
designed by Francesca Sundsten and Chris Zander for Wax Trax!/TVT Records

[1]*Nihil*—nothingness

7. Graphic Design

Marks

(*a*) Discuss this example of graphic design by referring to imagery, colour and type. What do you think the design communicates about the band, the music and the target market?

10

(*b*) Select **two** graphic designers whose work is from different periods or in different styles. Choose examples of work by these designers and show how their methods of communication differ, by referring to at least **two** of the following:

image, text, layout, visual impact, technology.

20

Explain why they are considered to be important graphic designers.

SECTION 2—DESIGN STUDIES (continued)

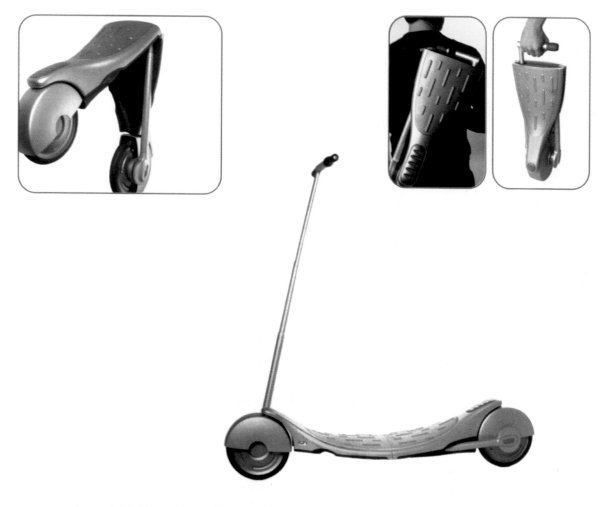

Scoot foldable, carbon fibre and aluminium scooter by Fuseproject (2000)

The scooter is propelled by hydrogen fuel without harming the environment.

Marks

8. **Product Design**

(*a*) What, in your opinion, are the main attractions and/or disadvantages of this scooter design? Discuss fully, giving reasons for your conclusions. **10**

(*b*) Product designers are constantly trying to meet the demands of an ever-changing market place. Choose **two** product designers, working in different periods or styles, who have demonstrated that they have met this challenge. Referring to specific examples of their work, explain why they are important designers. **20**

[Turn over

SECTION 2—DESIGN STUDIES (continued)

Domestic Interior, Standen, Sussex, England designed by Philip Webb (1892–94)

Marks

9. Interior Design

(a) Discuss the elements used by the designer to create this interior typical of the period. What are your views of his use of space and furnishings? How does the interior differ from a living/sitting room of today? **10**

(b) Select **two** interior designers who work in different periods or in contrasting styles. Refer to examples of their work, and show how *materials, working methods* and *changing fashions* have enabled them to develop new and exciting interior spaces. Explain why they are regarded as influential designers. **20**

SECTION 2—DESIGN STUDIES (continued)

Clear Channel Adshel—Enthoven Line Trainshelter (with public phone) (circa 2000)
designed by Enthoven Associates

Marks

10. Environmental/Architectural Design

(a) Highlight the main issues to be considered by the designer(s) in the development of this "street design". How successful is the design? Give reasons for your views.

10

(b) Select **two** environmental/architectural designers who work in different periods or whose styles are contrasting.

Compare and contrast typical work by each of them by referring to the following:

materials,   working methods,   influences,   aesthetics.

Why are they important designers?

20

[Turn over

SECTION 2—DESIGN STUDIES (continued)

Backpiece and Handpiece in white pewter and buffalo leather by Articular (1996)

Marks

11. Jewellery Design

(a) What do you think the design team is communicating through these jewellery designs? How practical are these ideas and when might they be worn? What are your personal thoughts about this approach to jewellery design?　**10**

(b) Select **two** jewellery designers who work in contrasting styles or are from different periods. Discuss why they are regarded as innovative and influential designers by referring to at least **two** of the following:

function,　use of materials,　techniques,　aesthetics,　technology.

Refer to examples of their work in your answer.　**20**

SECTION 2—DESIGN STUDIES (continued)

Personal Protection Unit designed by Edward Harber (2003)

This suit is made from Kevlar, a strong, synthetic, protective material.

Marks

12. Textile Design

(a) Discuss this motorcycle suit by referring to the key design issues considered by the designer. Can it be justified as a fashion item? Give reasons for your answer.

10

(b) Choose **two** fashion/textile designers whose styles are contrasting or who work in different periods. With reference to specific examples of their work, show how their distinctive approach to design has made them important and influential figures in their field.

20

[END OF QUESTION PAPER]

[BLANK PAGE]

[BLANK PAGE]

X003/301

NATIONAL
QUALIFICATIONS
2006

ART AND DESIGN
HIGHER
Paper 1
Practical Assignment

The Practical Examinations for the 2006 examination diet may take place at the centre's discretion on the most convenient date in the period from Monday 24 April until Friday 5 May inclusive.

Time allowed: 3 hours

50 marks are assigned to this paper.

Maximum sizes: Two-dimensional work: A2.
Three-dimensional work: 30 cm in greatest dimension.

Any medium except oil paint may be used.

SCOTTISH
QUALIFICATIONS
AUTHORITY

GENERAL INSTRUCTIONS

Base your work for the Practical Assignment on your Expressive Activity folio **or** your Design Activity folio.

In the examination room you may refer to your:

• Design **or** Expressive Folio of work

• Practical Assignment Form

You may use any three-dimensional source materials identified in the folio you have selected.

You will be allowed up to 20 minutes after the examination to assemble your work on the maximum number of sheets (2 × A2 sheets).

This extension time is not to be used for producing examination work.

Note: Copying of drawings and/or photographs from your folio by means such as TRACING, LIGHT BOXES, DIGITAL CAMERAS and PHOTOCOPYING **will not be permitted during the examination**. This exclusion also includes the use of computers and images and information copied from folios and stored on disk and/or CD.

Select **either** SECTION A **or** SECTION B.

SECTION A

Expressive Activity

Task

You should produce practical work which demonstrates your ability to develop and/or refine work carried out in your Expressive folio. This could take the form of new and further developments from your stimulus and might include extending ideas leading to alternative outcome(s) not fully explored within the work of your folio.

Remember that work produced for this Assignment should relate directly to your EXPRESSIVE folio theme and must develop, not copy, work already done. Further investigative work, such as analytical drawing, is not appropriate in this Assignment.

The following suggestions are provided to help you get started:

• produce work based on the stimulus or sources used by you but not fully explored in the work of your Expressive folio

• produce work which emphasises a different style or approach to your chosen theme.

Work should be on a maximum of **two** A2 sheets or equivalent three-dimensional work. You may use any suitable media, materials or process.

SECTION B

Design Activity

Task

You should produce practical work which demonstrates an alternative approach or approaches to work carried out in your Design folio. This could take the form of new and further developments from your brief and might include extending Design ideas not fully explored within the work of your folio.

Remember that work produced for this Assignment should relate to your DESIGN brief and Design folio and must develop, not copy, work already done. Further investigative work, such as analytical drawing, is not appropriate in this Assignment.

The following suggestions are provided to help you get started:

• develop Design ideas which you considered but did not fully explore in the work of your Design folio

• reconsider your solution and suggest further modifications and/or changes to improve it.

Work should be on a maximum of **two** A2 sheets or equivalent three-dimensional work. You may use any suitable media, materials or process.

[END OF QUESTION PAPER]

[BLANK PAGE]

X003/302

NATIONAL QUALIFICATIONS 2006	THURSDAY, 25 MAY 1.00PM – 3.00PM	ART AND DESIGN HIGHER Paper 2

There are **two** sections to this paper, Section 1—Art Studies; and Section 2—Design Studies.

Each section is worth 40 marks.

Candidates should attempt questions as follows:

In SECTION 1 answer **ONE full question** (parts (*a*) and (*b*)) and **ONE part (*a*) only** of any other question

and

In SECTION 2 answer **ONE full question** (parts (*a*) and (*b*)) and **ONE part (*a*) only** of any other question.

You may use sketches to illustrate your answers.

SECTION 1—ART STUDIES

Instructions

Answer **ONE full question**, (parts (*a*) and (*b*)), and **ONE part (*a*) only** of any other question.

John Bellany *My Father* (1966) oil on board (122 × 91·5 cm)

Marks

1. Portraiture

(*a*) Discuss the methods used by the artist to reveal aspects of his father's character to us. Comment on composition, use of visual elements and handling of paint. Explain your personal reaction to this portrait.　　　**10**

(*b*) Discuss contrasting approaches to portraiture by **two** artists from different movements or periods. Comment on their choice of subjects, styles and working methods. Explain why you consider your artists to be important.　　　**20**

SECTION 1—ART STUDIES (continued)

Sebastião Salgado, *Dispute between Serra Pelada gold mine workers and military police*,
Brazil, 1986

Marks

2. Figure Composition

(a) Discuss the composition of this photograph. Comment on the relationships between the figures. How successfully does the photograph capture the tension of the situation?

10

(b) Discuss the use of the human figure as subject matter. Refer to the work of **two** artists from different movements or periods. Compare the working methods and styles of these artists and comment on their success and importance.

20

[Turn over

SECTION 1—ART STUDIES (continued)

Henri Matisse   *Goldfish and Palette* (1914) oil on canvas (146 × 112 cm)

Marks

3. Still Life

(*a*) Discuss how **two or more** of the following contribute to the impact of this painting:

composition;   *abstraction;*   *visual elements;*   *media handling.*

What thoughts or feelings are communicated to you when you view this painting?   **10**

(*b*) Discuss examples of still life by **two** artists from different movements or periods. Comment on their choice of subject matter, working methods and style. Explain why you consider them to be influential artists.   **20**

SECTION 1—ART STUDIES (continued)

Christo and Jeanne-Claude *Wrapped Coast* (1969). The coastline of Little Bay, Australia, wrapped in fabric and rope. © Christo 1969

Marks

4. Natural Environment

(*a*) Discuss the methods used by the artists to create this example of Land Art[1]. Comment on the use of materials, scale and choice of site. Explain your personal reaction to this work.

10

(*b*) Discuss the working methods of **two** artists from different movements or periods who have taken inspiration from the natural environment. Referring to examples, comment on their different approaches and styles. Explain why you consider them to be important artists.

20

[1]*Land Art*—a type of art in which the artist uses actual land, earth and stones combined with other objects.

[Turn over

SECTION 1—ART STUDIES (continued)

David Mach *Here to Stay* (1990) Installation[1] using recycled newspapers.

[1]*Installation*—a form of art in which objects, images, words and video are often used together in a gallery or other space to communicate the artist's message. This installation has been created from 180 tons of surplus daily newspapers.

Marks

5. **Built Environment**

(a) What is your opinion of this installation? In your answer comment on methods of construction, scale and choice of materials.   **10**

(b) Discuss the working methods of **two** artists from different movements or periods. Referring to examples within the theme of the Built Environment, comment on their choice of subject matter and differences in approach. Explain how the examples are typical of their styles.   **20**

Goya   *Colossus*[1] (1808–1812) oil on canvas (116 × 105 cm)

[1]*Colossus*—larger than life figure

Marks

6.   Fantasy and Imagination

(a)   Discuss the composition of this painting.   Comment on the use of visual
elements and the methods used by the artist to communicate a feeling of
terror.   What are your personal thoughts about this work?   **10**

(b)   Discuss **two** artists from different movements or periods whose work within
this theme interests you.   Referring to examples, discuss the methods used by
the artists to communicate their ideas.   Explain why you consider them to be
influential artists.   **20**

[Turn over

Instructions

Answer **ONE full question**, (parts (*a*) and (*b*)), and **ONE part (*a*) only** of any other question.

Travel poster by Alphons Mucha (1897)

Marks

7. Graphic Design

(*a*) Discuss the effectiveness of this poster design with particular reference to its imagery, layout and use of colour. In your opinion, how does this poster differ from modern posters?

10

(*b*) Choose **two** graphic designers working in different periods or styles and compare their methods of visual communication. Identify key aspects of their work and state why they are regarded as important designers.

20

SECTION 2—DESIGN STUDIES (continued)

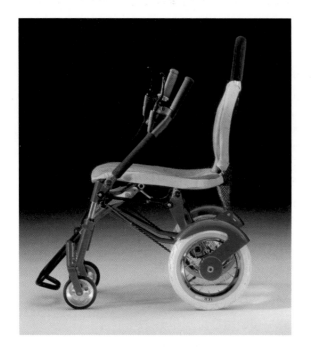
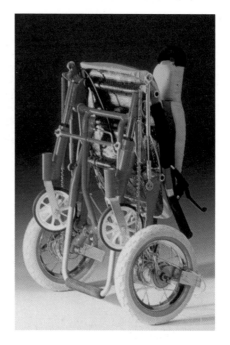

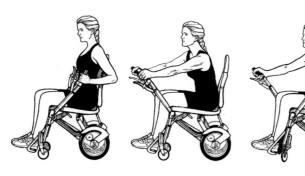

moving forward   *turning*

New Move Wheelchair designed by Douglas Clarkson (1994). *The chair is lightweight, foldable and powered by the user moving the handle bars in a forward/backward movement.*

Marks

8. Product Design

(a) Style, function and target market are important considerations in the development of a design concept. Comment on each of these in relation to Douglas Clarkson's wheelchair design. In your opinion how successful is the design and why?

10

(b) Select **two** designers working in different periods or styles. With reference to examples of their work, discuss how they have contributed to the development of everyday products. Which of the **two** do you consider to be the more important designer and why?

20

[Turn over

SECTION 2—DESIGN STUDIES (continued)

Dance Club designed by Graven Images (1999)

Marks

9. Interior Design

(*a*) Identify the key design issues that have been considered in the designing of this contemporary interior. With particular reference to the use of lighting and space, consider how effective the designers' ideas are.

10

(*b*) Select **two** interior designers who work in different periods or styles and comment on their importance. Compare their approaches to the designing of interiors by referring to their use of at least **two** of the following: lighting, materials, space, colour, form, influences.

20

SECTION 2—DESIGN STUDIES (continued)

Lloyds Building, London designed by architect Richard Rogers (1986)

Marks

10. Environmental/Architectural Design

(a) How has Richard Rogers's use of materials, forms and structures made this building stand out from those in its immediate surroundings? Do you consider that his vision for this contemporary building has been successful? Give reasons for your answer.   **10**

(b) Select **two** architectural/environmental designers working in different periods. With reference to at least **two** examples of their work, show how their use of materials and working methods have contributed to the development of architecture. Explain why they are considered to be important designers.   **20**

SECTION 2—DESIGN STUDIES (continued)

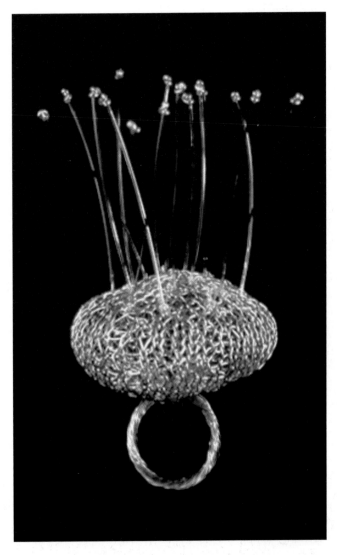 

Regeneration Ring, knitted nylon   *Thistle Ring*, woven nylon

Rings by Nora Fok (1999)

Marks

11. Jewellery Design

(a) Discuss Nora Fok's choice of materials, working methods and sources of inspiration for these jewellery pieces. Which target audience do you think that these pieces are aimed at, and how practical do you consider them to be as fashion accessories? Justify your answer.   **10**

(b) "Jewellery designers produce accessories which compliment the work of the fashion designer." Do you agree? Discuss this statement with reference to the work of **two** jewellery designers from different periods or styles. Explain their contribution to the development of jewellery.   **20**

SECTION 2—DESIGN STUDIES (continued)

Costume for *the Blue God* by Léon Bakst for the Ballet Russes,
Russian State ballet (1912)

Marks

12. Textile Design

(a) Discuss the ways in which Léon Bakst has used shape, pattern, colour and applied decoration to create this costume. How practical do you think the design is, and how might its appearance enhance the ballet production?   **10**

(b) Refer to the work of **two** fashion and/or textile designers, working in different periods or styles. Show how they have experimented with new and/or unusual materials and working methods in the development of fashion and/or textile design. Explain why they have been influential in this field of design.   **20**

[END OF QUESTION PAPER]

[BLANK PAGE]

The following changes to the Art & Design Higher examination apply in and after 2007.

- There is no longer a Practical Assignment examination.
- The Higher question paper has been reduced by half an hour as there are fewer questions to answer. Candidates are required to answer one FULL question parts (a) and (b) in each Section. Previously, candidates were required to answer an additional part (a) from each section. Each section is now worth **30** marks instead of 40 marks.

[BLANK PAGE]

X223/301

NATIONAL
QUALIFICATIONS
2007

THURSDAY, 31 MAY
1.00 PM – 2.30 PM

ART AND DESIGN
HIGHER

There are **two** sections to this paper, Section 1—Art Studies; and Section 2—Design Studies.

Each section is worth 30 marks.

Candidates should attempt questions as follows:

In SECTION 1 answer **ONE full question** (parts (*a*) **and** (*b*))

and

In SECTION 2 answer **ONE full question** (parts (*a*) **and** (*b*)).

You may use sketches to illustrate your answers.

SCOTTISH
QUALIFICATIONS
AUTHORITY

SECTION 1—ART STUDIES

Instructions

Read your selected question and notes on the illustration carefully.

Answer **ONE full question from this section**: parts (*a*) and (*b*).

Gustav Klimt, *Portrait of Adele Bloch-Bauer* (1907)
oil paint and gold leaf on canvas (138 × 138 cm)

Marks

1. **Portraiture**

(*a*) Discuss the methods used by Klimt to portray the character of the sitter. Comment on **at least two** of the following:

composition;   colour;   pattern;   pose.

What is your opinion of the painting?   10

(*b*) Select **two** artists from different movements or periods. Compare and contrast portraiture by each of them by referring to:

subject matter;   styles and working methods.

Why are these artists considered important in the development of portraiture?   20

SECTION 1—ART STUDIES (continued)

Richard Hamilton, *Swinging London 67*, (1968–69)
oil and silkscreen[1] on canvas (67 × 85 cm)

[1]Silkscreen—a printing process used by the artist to reproduce a newspaper photograph onto a large canvas. Oil paint was then added to complete the work.

Marks

2. Figure Composition

(a) Discuss the artist's choice of subject matter. In doing so, comment on **at least two** of the following:

composition; colour; tone; working method.

What is your opinion of the picture? **10**

(b) Referring to examples of figure composition by **two** artists from different movements or periods, explain why you consider the works to be successful. To what extent do you think these artists are influential in the development of figure composition? **20**

[Turn over

SECTION 1—ART STUDIES (continued)

Raymond Han, *Still Life with Orange Tin and Produce Containers* (1992–93)
oil on canvas (71 × 112 cm)

Marks

3. Still Life

(a) Discuss the composition of this still life painting. Comment on the artist's choice of subject matter, use of visual elements and media handling. What is your opinion of this painting? **10**

(b) Referring to examples of still life by **two** artists from different movements or periods, explain why you consider the works to be successful. How important are the artists in the development of still life? Discuss your answer. **20**

SECTION 1—ART STUDIES (continued)

Thomas Joshua Cooper, *Archipelago*[1]*—North Atlantic Ocean* (2002)
photograph (43 × 60 cm)

[1]*Archipelago*—a group of small islands

Marks

4. **Natural Environment**

(*a*) Discuss the visual impact of this photograph. In doing so, refer to **at least two** of the following:

tone;   *composition*;   *detail*.

Why do you think Cooper was attracted to this subject matter?   **10**

(*b*) Select **two** artists from different movements or periods. Referring to examples of their work, explain the differences and/or similarities in their responses to the natural environment. Why are they considered important artists?   **20**

[Turn over

SECTION 1—ART STUDIES (continued)

Sir Robin Philipson, *Cathedral Interior* (1978) oil on canvas (127 × 102 cm)

Marks

5. Built Environment

(a) Discuss the artist's personal response to this interior. Refer to **at least two** of the following:

colour; *shape*; *pattern*; *composition*.

What is your opinion of the painting? **10**

(b) Discuss examples of work, based on the built environment, by **two** artists from different movements or periods. Explain the methods used by the artists to create their work. To what extent are the examples typical of the artists' style or associated movement? **20**

SECTION 1—ART STUDIES (continued)

Antony Gormley, *Angel of the North* (1998) Cor-ten steel[1] (20 metres high, 54 metres wide)

[1]Cor-ten steel—a type of steel which oxidises naturally to an orange-brown colour but despite its rusted appearance is actually resistant to corrosion.

This sculpture stands on a hillside above the town of Gateshead beside a busy motorway.

Marks

6. Fantasy and Imagination

(a) Discuss to what extent you consider this to be a successful sculpture for this specific site. In doing so, refer to the scale of the work and the artist's use of symbolism. **10**

(b) Select **two** artists from different movements or periods whose work is within the theme of fantasy and imagination. Referring to examples of work, discuss the methods used by the artists to communicate their ideas. Explain to what extent the artists are influential in the development of this type of artwork. **20**

[Turn over

SECTION 2—DESIGN STUDIES

Instructions

Read your selected question and notes on the illustration carefully.

Answer **ONE full question from this section**: parts **(a)** and **(b)**.

Poster Design by A M Cassandre (mid 1920s)

Marks

7. Graphic Design

(a) What message is Cassandre communicating through this poster? Discuss his treatment of this design by referring to **at least two** of the following:

imagery; *colour*; *text*; *layout*.

What is your opinion of this design? Give reasons.　　　　　　**10**

(b) Select **two** graphic designers from different periods or of contrasting styles. Discuss why they are considered to be important. By referring to specific examples of their work, show how they have introduced new approaches to this area of design.　　　　　　**20**

SECTION 2—DESIGN STUDIES (continued)

Sony Portable TV, designed by Sony Design Centre (1959).
Casing made from plastic and metal. Screen 46 cm (18 in), weight 6 kg.

Marks

8. Product Design

(a) Why do you think this product was considered to be ahead of its time? How does it compare with similar products of today? What is your opinion of this design?

10

(b) Select **two** important product designers who have worked in different periods or in contrasting styles. By referring to their work, show how they have responded to the changing needs of society. Why are they regarded as significant designers?

20

[Turn over

SECTION 2—DESIGN STUDIES (continued)

Debating Chamber, Scottish Parliament Building, designed by Enric Miralles (2003)

Marks

9. Interior Design

(a) How well do you think this interior fulfils its function? In your answer, refer to Mirales' use of **at least two** of the following:

space; *use of materials*; *structure*; *form*; *light*; *colour*.

What is your personal view of this interior space?

10

(b) Choose **two** interior designers from different periods or of contrasting styles. With reference to some of their best work, discuss how their new approaches have contributed to the development of interior design.

20

SECTION 2—DESIGN STUDIES (continued)

Falling Water designed by Frank Lloyd Wright (1935–37).
Materials used include steel, stone and reinforced concrete.

Marks

10. Environmental/Architectural Design

(*a*) Discuss the key architectural features of this dwelling house. What is your opinion of this design? Justify your views in terms of its strengths and/or weaknesses.

10

(*b*) Architects are often presented with opportunities to change the face of the environment. Select **two** architects from different periods or whose approach to design is different. Show, by discussing examples of their work, why they have made important architectural statements.

20

[Turn over

SECTION 2—DESIGN STUDIES (continued)

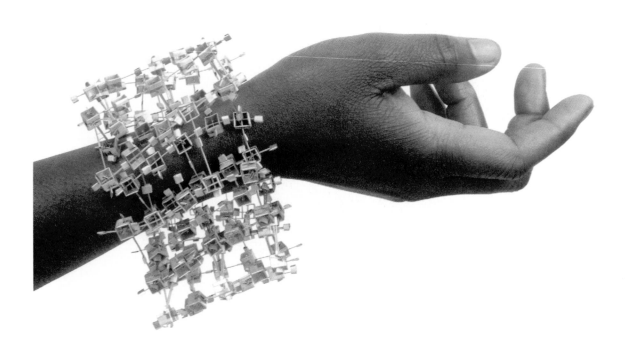

Another Life designed by Marie Asbjørnsen (2003) from recycled aluminium cans
and steel wire.

Marks

11. Jewellery Design

(a) Comment on this jewellery design in terms of the designer's use of materials,
handling of form and the wearability of the piece. What are your views on the
use of recycled materials to create jewellery? **10**

(b) Choose **two** distinguished jewellery designers from different periods or of
different styles. Refer to examples of their work and discuss how influences
and use of materials have inspired them. Explain why these **two** designers are
highly regarded. **20**

SECTION 2—DESIGN STUDIES (continued)

Outfit created by Saksit Pisalasupones (2005)

Marks

12. Textile/Fashion Design

(*a*) Comment as fully as you can on this outfit by referring to key design issues. Do you think the designer intends it to be taken seriously? Give reasons for your answer.

10

(*b*) Choose **two** important textile and/or fashion designers from different periods or of contrasting styles. Select examples of their work and discuss how they have created successful designs. Why are they regarded as important in this area of design?

20

[END OF QUESTION PAPER]

[BLANK PAGE]

[BLANK PAGE]

X223/301

NATIONAL
QUALIFICATIONS
2008

TUESDAY, 3 JUNE
1.00 PM – 2.30 PM

ART AND DESIGN
HIGHER

There are **two** sections to this paper, Section 1—Art Studies; and Section 2—Design Studies.

Each section is worth 30 marks.

Candidates should attempt questions as follows:

In SECTION 1 answer **ONE full question** (parts (*a*) **and** (*b*))

and

In SECTION 2 answer **ONE full question** (parts (*a*) **and** (*b*)).

You may use sketches to illustrate your answers.

SECTION 1—ART STUDIES

Instructions

Read your selected question and notes on the illustration carefully.

Answer **ONE full question from this section**: parts *(a)* and *(b)*.

Portrait of the Journalist Sylvia Von Harden (1926) by Otto Dix,
oil and tempera on wood (120 × 88 cm)

Marks

1. Portraiture

(a) How successfully does Otto Dix communicate Sylvia von Harden's personality
in the painting? In your response, refer to **at least two** of the following:

pose; composition; use of visual elements; media handling.

What is your personal opinion of this painting?

10

(b) Compare examples of work by **two** artists from different movements or
periods whose approaches to portraiture are contrasting. Explain why you
consider the artists to be important in the development of portraiture.

20

SECTION 1—ART STUDIES (continued)

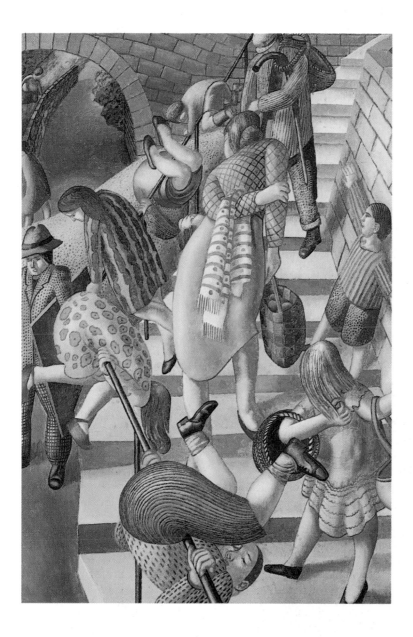

The Glen, Port Glasgow (1952) by Sir Stanley Spencer,
oil on canvas (76·2 × 50·9 cm)

Marks

2. Figure Composition

(a) Discuss the composition of this painting. Comment on the use of **at least two** of the following:

perspective; pattern; line; colour.

What is your opinion of the painting?

10

(b) Discuss examples of figure composition by **two** artists from different movements or periods. Comment on the differences and/or similarities in their styles. Explain why they are considered to be important artists.

20

[Turn over

SECTION 1—ART STUDIES (continued)

Still Life: Autumn Fashion (1978) by Patrick Caulfield,
acrylic on canvas (61 × 76·2 cm)

Marks

3. Still Life

(a) Discuss the methods used by the artist to create visual impact in this painting.
Refer to his use of visual elements. Explain your personal opinion of this
approach to still life painting.

10

(b) Compare examples of still life by **two** artists from different movements or
periods. Explain the differences and/or similarities in their choice of subject
matter and treatment of it. Why do you consider the artists to be important?

20

SECTION 1—ART STUDIES (continued)

The Storm (1890) by William McTaggart,
oil on canvas (122 × 183 cm)

Marks

4. Natural Environment

(a) Discuss the methods used by McTaggart to express in paint the effect of weather on this coastal scene. What is your opinion of the painting?

10

(b) Compare examples of work by **two** artists from different movements or periods. Your comparison should discuss their different approaches and responses to the natural environment. Explain why you consider the artists to be important in the development of this theme.

20

[Turn over

SECTION 1—ART STUDIES (continued)

Place du Tertre (1911) by Maurice Utrillo,
oil on canvas (50·2 × 73 cm)

Marks

5. Built Environment

(a) Discuss the composition of this painting. Comment on Utrillo's use of **at least two** of the following:

colour; *texture*; *shape*; *perspective*.

What does the painting make you think or feel about this location?

10

(b) Discuss examples of work inspired by the built environment by **two** artists from different movements or periods. Comment on their choice of subject, working methods and style. Explain why you consider the artists to be important.

20

SECTION 1—ART STUDIES (continued)

The Great Red Dragon and the Woman Clothed in Sun (1806–1809) by William Blake,
watercolour on paper (42 × 34·3 cm)

Marks

6. Fantasy and Imagination

(*a*) Discuss the composition of this painting. Comment on the methods used by Blake to create this powerful image. What is your opinion of this painting? **10**

(*b*) Discuss examples of work within this theme by **two** artists from different movements or periods. Explain the methods used by the artists to communicate their ideas. Why do you consider these artists to be important in the development of fantasy and imagination? **20**

SECTION 2—DESIGN STUDIES

Instructions

Read your selected question and notes on the illustration carefully.

Answer **ONE full question from this section**: parts **(a)** and **(b)**.

Tekken 4, cover design for Sony PlayStation 2 game (1997)

Marks

7. Graphic Design

(a) Comment on the use of technology in this graphic work. What does it communicate about the product and the target market? What is your personal opinion of this style of graphic design? **10**

(b) Choose **two** important graphic designers from different periods or who work in different styles. By referring to examples of their work, show how they communicate with their target audience. Explain why they are highly regarded in this area of design. **20**

SECTION 2—DESIGN STUDIES (continued)

Teapot designed by Marianne Brandt (1924).
Materials: silver with hardwood handle.

Marks

8. Product Design

(a) Discuss the form and functionality of this design. What would have been the target market for this product in 1924? Compare it with a teapot you have used.

10

(b) Select **two** product designers from different periods or who work in contrasting styles. Refer to examples of their work and explain why their products are popular with the consumer. Why are these two designers acknowledged as important product designers?

20

[Turn over

SECTION 2—DESIGN STUDIES (continued)

Rogano Restaurant, designed by Weddell and Inglis (1937)

Marks

9. Interior Design

(a) Comment on the design elements that contribute to the style and mood of this interior. Who might use the restaurant and do you think the interior would add to the experience? Justify your views.

10

(b) Select **two** interior designers from different periods or whose style is contrasting. Discuss specific examples of their work, which demonstrate why they are regarded as innovative and important designers.

20

SECTION 2—DESIGN STUDIES (continued)

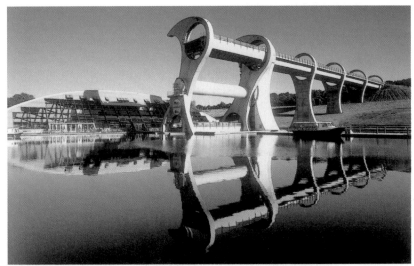

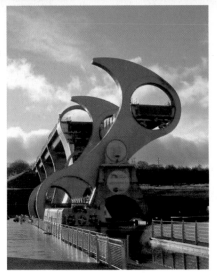

The Falkirk Wheel, designed by RMJM architects (2002).

The design enables boats to be raised and lowered between the high level canal and the lower canal.

Marks

10. Environmental/Architectural Design

(a) Discuss how this design relates to its immediate environment. Refer to **at least two** of the following:

scale; *form*; *function*.

Do you regard this to be a worthwhile design solution? Give reasons.

10

(b) Select **two** environmental/architectural designers from different periods or who work in different styles. Refer to specific examples of their work and show how they have introduced new ideas and working methods in their designs. Why are they regarded as important in the development of this type of design?

20

SECTION 2—DESIGN STUDIES (continued)

Tiara and Brooch, designed for the Empress Eugenie by Gabriel Lemonnier (1853).
Materials: gold, pearls and diamonds.

Marks

11. Jewellery Design

(*a*) Discuss these jewellery pieces by referring to **at least two** of the following:

craftsmanship; *use of materials*; *fitness for purpose*; *aesthetics*.

What do they say about the status of the wearer? Would they be appropriate for today's fashion market? Give reasons for your views.

10

(*b*) Choose **two** important jewellery designers who are from different periods or whose approach to design is contrasting. Show how they have used their skills and creative talents to produce work for their target audience(s). Use specific examples of their work to support your comment. State why they are highly regarded designers.

20

SECTION 2—DESIGN STUDIES (continued)

Gentleman's outfit by unknown French designer (circa 1800)

Marks

12. Textile/Fashion Design

(a) What is your opinion of this outfit? Refer to **at least two** of the following in support of your opinions:

shape; detailing; accessories; functionality.

Compare this outfit with today's formal wear for men.

10

(b) Select **two** innovative textile or fashion designers from different periods or who work in different styles. By referring to important influences, discuss examples of their work. Explain why they are highly regarded designers.

20

[END OF QUESTION PAPER]

[BLANK PAGE]

[BLANK PAGE]

[BLANK PAGE]

[BLANK PAGE]

[BLANK PAGE]

[BLANK PAGE]

Acknowledgements

Leckie and Leckie is grateful to the copyright holders, as credited, for permission to use their material:
Diego on My Mind (Self-Portrait as Tehuana Indian) by Frido Kahlo © 2006 Banco de México Diego Rivera & Frido Kahlo Museums Trust. Av.
Cinco de Mayo No. 2, Col. Centro, Del. Cuauhtémoc 06059, México, D.F.
(2005 P2 Q1);
The Dance by Paula Rego, © Tate, London 2006/Paula Rego (2005 P2 Q2);
The Wheatfield by Raol Duffy © ADAGP, Paris and DACS, London 2005/ Tate, London 2006 (2005 P2 Q4);
Market Church at Evening by Lyonel Feininger © DACS, London 2005 (2005 P2 Q5);
My Father by John Bellamy © National Galleries of Scotland/The Bridgeman Art Library (2006 P2 Q1);
Dispute between Serra Pelada gold mine workers and military police by Sebastião Salgado © nb pictures (2006 P2 Q2);
Goldfish and Palette by Henri Matisse. DIGITAL IMAGE © 2007 The Museum of Modern Art/Scala, Florence (2006 P2 Q3);
Colossus by Francisco Goya © Photo SCALA, Florence (2006 P2 Q6);
Dance Club by Graven Images © Keith Hunter/Arcblue (2006 P2 Q9);
Lloyds Building, London © Life File Photographic Library (2006 P2 Q10); Portrait of Adele Bloch-Bauer by Gustav Klimt © AKG Images (2007 P2 Q1);

Swinging London by Richard Hamilton © Richard Hamilton. All Rights Reserved, DACS 2007. Leckie and Leckie has paid DACS' visual creators for the use of their artistic works. (2007 P2 Q2);
Poster Design by A M Cassandre © MOURON . CASSANDRE. Lic Proposal. www.cassandre.fr (2007 P2 Q7);
A photograph by Sakchai Lalit © PA Photos (2007 P2 Q12);
Portrait of the Journalist Sylvia von Harden by Otto Dix © DACS, London 2008 (2008 P2 Q1);
The Glen, Port Glasgow by Sir Stanley Spencer @ Glasgow Museums. Licensor www.scran.ac.uk (2008 P2 Q2);
The Storm by William Mc Taggart @ Dundee City Council - Arts and Heritage. Licensor www.scran.ac.uk (2008 P2 Q4);
Picture of Rogano Restaurant designed by Weddel and Inlgis @University of Strathclyde. Licensor www.Scran.ac.uk;
Place du Tertre by Maurice Utrillo © Jean FABRIS 2008 (2008 P2 Q5);
The Great Red Dragon and the Woman Clothed in Sun by William Blake @ Brooklyn Museum (2008 P2 Q6).

The following companies/individuals have very generously given permission to reproduce their copyright material free of charge:
Still Life with Vase of Hydrangeas and Ranunculus by Henri Fantin- Latour © Toledo Museum of Art (2005 P2 Q3);
Leviathan Elegy by Will Maclean © Will Maclean (2005 P2 Q6);
Scoot Foldable Scooter by Fuseproject © Fuseproject (2005 P2 Q8); Domestic Interior by Philip Webb © The Quarto Group Inc. (2005 P2 Q9);
Clear Channel Adshel by Enthoven Associates © Enthoven Associates (2005 P2 Q10);
Wrapped Coast by Christo and Jeanne-Claude © Christo 1969 (2006 P2 Q4);
Here to Stay by David Mach © Alan Wylie/Tramway (2006 P2 Q5);
Rings by Nora Fok © Crafts Council (2006 P2 Q11);
Costume for the Blue God by Léon Bakst © National Gallery of Australia (2006 P2 Q12);
Still Life with Orange Tin and Produce Containers by Raymond Han © Raymond Han, courtesy of Forum Gallery, New York, NY (2007 P2 Q3);
Archipelago - North Atlantic Ocean by Thomas Joshua Cooper © Thomas Joshua Cooper (2007 P2 Q4);
Cathedral Interior by Sir Robin Philipson reproduced by kind permission of The Royal Bank of Scotland © 2007 (2007 P2 Q5);
Another Life by Marie Asbjornsen © Crafts Council (2007 P2 Q11)